FOREWORD

Visitors to York enthuse about tl
remaining, and residents are p
architecture, but this book prese
vanished heritage. York still kee
but like any twentieth century c
buildings in between. For the most part York is poorer for the loss of so much that added to its character, and an often voiced regret is that few buildings of quality replace the old. But if the work of the architect and builder has vanished, that of the artist and photographer survives. The pictures also present an introduction to many of the topographical artists who have worked in York, and who have loved the ambience of the city. I hope you will enjoy seeing York as they knew it.

Darrell Buttery

The Duke of Buckingham's house once stood proudly on Bishophill. Now only street names recall its splendid presence.

The Old Deanery, pulled down in 1831, stood on the site now occupied by the Minster Song School. It was a building of considerable antiquity and scene of many notable events. In 1640 King Charles I was in York. To avoid summoning a Parliament, he convened a Great Council of the Peers of the Realm. They met in the Deanery, whose hall was specially hung with tapestry for the historic occasion. For several weeks the Council met there, and York can never before or since have had so many noblemen living within its walls. In 1789 the future George IV and his brother the Duke of York were entertained to dinner in the Deanery, which was 'borrowed' for the occasion by Earl Fitzwilliam. The Deanery built to replace this one, but on a different site, has also been demolished, giving way to a bland neo-Georgian house on yet another site.

When the Bagnio, or Turkish Bath, was demolished in 1924 York lost one of its historically most important buildings. This little baroque structure, painted here by W. J. Boddy, stood on a site behind Coney Street. The local historian, George Benson, describes how "one could sweat and bath and be cupped after the German fashion for 5s each. It was open from 7 a.m. to 9 p.m. Tuesdays and Fridays were reserved for women". But selling cleanliness did not pay in York, and by 1738 the Bagnio was in use as a printing office. Here York's most successful eighteenth century newspaper, The York Courant, was published, as well as the first Annual Racing Calendar. What would have made the Bagnio a literary shrine today is the fact that it could well have been where Laurence Sterne's 'Tristram Shandy' was first printed, in 1759.

One of the greatest mansions ever to grace York was Sir Thomas Ingram's house, a building standing by the Minster and not to be dwarfed by it. The present Dean's Park was the garden of the house, and descriptions that have come down to us make its disappearance as regrettable as that of the house. A traveller in 1634 called it 'a second paradise . . . rare gardens and curious long walkes, which were adorned with many kinds of beasts to the life, with most lively statues in several shapes and forms. A pleasant fair tennis court, a delightful large bowling-ground newlie made, curiously contrived fish-ponds; all which make up another sweet little citie. A place it is, so pleasant to all the sences as art and nature can make it.' In this 'rich mansion' King Charles the First lived during his long stay in York in 1642. This early nineteenth century sketch shows the once noble house in ruinous condition.

So many fine buildings, had they survived, could have found new uses. This spacious medieval hall behind the Shambles could have earned its keep in many ways, but sadly it came down some time in the 1950s. The drawing is by Ridsdale Tate, a York architect who spent much time recording the city in sketches and watercolours.

At the bottom of the facing page, looking like a proper castle, Francis Place's view is taken from the South West and shows York Castle as it was, long before it was reduced to only Clifford's Tower and a stretch of isolated walling. The top picture, a birdseye view by an unknown artist, looks at the view from the other side some forty years later. The handsome governor's house in the foreground has gone, along with its formal garden, and buildings by John Carr have replaced the two which flank the Debtors' Prison. Clifford's Tower is shown with the scars it received in 1684 when it nearly became a vanished building of York. Citizens resented the garrison housed there in the reign of James II, and there were threats to blow up 'the minced pie', as the tower was contemptuously called. An explosion of gunpowder blew off the roof in 1684 and so seriously damaged the building it was never used again.

A cheerful little wash drawing of Castlegate Postern, a feel of Italy come to York. The great gateway to the castle, approached by a drawbridge over the Foss, was blocked in 1708. It is shown in the middle of Francis Place's drawing on the facing page. Throughout the eighteenth century the principal entrance to the castle was through this narrow gate, seen here from the castle side looking through to Castlegate. Nothing in the view now remains.

Left

For centuries a feature of Micklegate was the gateway of Holy Trinity Priory. The shabby antiquity of its inner face, looking through to the street, was captured in this watercolour by the Victorian artist Francis Bedford. Remnants of the Priory and the grounds had survived until the middle of the nineteenth century, whereas today only part of the church stands. In 1854 the gateway was taken down, Priory Street formed, and the rest of the land developed.

Facing page

St Mary's Abbey would have been a much more substantial ruin had not our ancestors used its stone for major repair jobs on other buildings, including Beverley Minster. In this anonymous, rather unsure drawing at the top of the page, part of the nave and the whole of the North West aisle are shown as being intact. Now only the wall of the latter, famous backdrop for the Mystery Plays, remains.

The lower drawing, about the same date, shows the abbey remains from a different angle. It is possibly by the artist William Lodge, who was active in the early eighteenth century.

Before the Purey Cust Nursing Home this ancient property rambled over the site. In spite of later windows and doorway, the house itself probably had a pedigree going back to the Middle Ages. Fenton House, at the end of Precentor's Court, can be seen on the far left.

St. Thomas's Hospital, just outside Micklegate Bar, survived long enough to appear in the first hazy photographs of the city. Once the home of the Corpus Christi Guild, it was pulled down in 1862.

Left

Henry Cave was busy in the early years of the nineteenth century recording large tracts of the medieval and Elizabethan city before such inconvenient relics were swept away. Here is his view of Low Ousegate with the narrow hump of Ouse Bridge in the background. Not a single feature of the view survives.

Facing page

Looking as if it was caught dancing, this nursery-rhyme cottage snuggled up close to the inner face of Walmgate Bar. Ignoring the major monument for once, Henry Cave drew the cottage in 1808, making one wonder how many visual pleasures of York went unrecorded.

A house with a similar gable which once stood in Gillygate. George Nicholson, a prolific and gifted topographical artist working a little later than Cave, drew this strangely built property in one of his sketchbooks.

This decorative front, drawn by Henry Cave and looking like a bit of fairground art, once enlivened a facade in Stonegate. If we tried to do the same today what *would* the Planning Department say? The buildings survive, by the entry to Coffee Yard, but not the decoration.

We think of St. Saviourgate today as being a Georgian street with some unwelcome twentieth century intrusions, but it did have some earlier houses which survived till Victorian times and caught the eye of artists. G. H. Fowler Jones produced this watercolour of a typical jettied house of the Middle Ages.

Today the only attractive thing about Castle Mills Bridge is its name. It seems no more than a stretch of modern road, but in the past there was much more to recommend it. Mills had been situated in this area since the eleventh century. Later came St. George's Chapel where medieval kings of England worshipped on their frequent stays in York. This watercolour, by A. E. Wilkinson, shows the last range of buildings here, popularly known as St. George's Priory. They were demolished in the mid-nineteenth century, but the land is still known as St. George's Fields.

One of York's most recorded sights was old Ouse Bridge, built in the thirteenth century and replaced by the present structure in 1820. It was more than just a bridge, for St. William's Chapel stood at the Micklegate end, and across the road from it was the dampest of the city's gaols. In the early days there were shops and houses along its full length.

St. William's Chapel being reduced to a vanished building of York. Henry Cave made a number of etchings of the chapel for inclusion in his book 'Antiquities of York' published in 1813.

Even familiar monuments aren't what they used to be. Who would recognise this as the inner face of Bootham Bar? The sketch was made in 1827 by George Nicholson, just a few years before the barbican was removed and at a time when the entire structure was under threat. The Bar has since been restored to look more truly medieval. The figure in the niche represented Ebraucus, legendary founder of York a thousand years before Christ. There had been a statue of Ebraucus in York since medieval times, but this one was placed here in 1738.

This was the inner face of Micklegate Bar, likewise unrecognisable to modern eyes, with dwellings pressed up against it and a house extension clinging to its back. The artist, R. Douglas, seems to have been better at proportioning buildings rather than people.

In 1803 the artist Nattes did this squared drawing of the Old Market Place, which had a character not unlike that of a country town. Little remains of the view other than the church of All Saints, and that much truncated. The creation of Parliament Street and Piccadilly swept away two intimate market places and produced a town centre shopping area so nondescript that the York Chamber of Trade and Commerce held a competition in 1975 for suggestions to improve it. The old market cross was erected in 1672, providing shelter below and a room above, though the edifice was 'ill-executed' according to York historian Francis Drake. The following year the turret and weather vane were added 'and the appearance of the building was greatly improved' according to another local historian, William Hargrove. It came down in 1813.

The other market building was this handsome structure in St. Sampson's Square, then called Thursday Market. For centuries there had been a market hall here but this one, erected in 1705, was to be the last on the site. This time the opinions of the two historians seem to have been reversed. Drake calls it "a beautiful and useful structure"; Hargrove says "its beauty may be questioned." Besides its obvious use as a shelter for market folk, the upper room almost from the beginning served as a theatre before there was a Theatre Royal, and later it survived as "a highly respectable Commercial Academy". It lasted only two years longer than the market cross.

A precedent was set in Tudor times for pulling down medieval churches in York, and their removal was continued in the nineteenth and twentieth centuries right up to 1963. The picture shows one such medieval loss, St. Lawrence's Church, outside Walmgate Bar. Only the tower remains, a frail structure standing near to the black mass of the Victorian church built to replace its medieval namesake.

Francis Bedford's watercolour of 1841 depicts the old church of St. Maurice, off Monkgate, highlighting its distinctive roofline. The church stood until 1876, when it was replaced by a larger Victorian one, which has now given way to a featureless office block and shaven lawns.

Everything in this Victorian view of York has gone. The half-timbered houses on the right are looked at in more detail on page 68. The buildings on the left are now replaced by Marks and Spencers. The Old George Hotel in the background went in 1957 to make way for the unlovely Stonebow. St Crux, the finest fifteenth century church in York, was pulled down in 1886 and its handsome monuments crowded into a little church hall on the site. The picture is a well known one, coming from Monkhouse and Bedford's book 'The Churches of York'.

This later Victorian painting of St. Crux, by H. Richardson, is taken from the Shambles. The tower, bereft now of its urns, was erected in 1697 and considered by Drake to be 'handsome'. A century later Davies thought otherwise: "the unsightly cupola and its tower of brick, which now deforms the church of St. Crux, bespeaks a tasteless period." The view was painted in 1881, the year in which the church was closed for public worship because it had become so unsafe. In 1884, in a characteristically Victorian way, demolition preparatory to 'restoration' began. There wasn't enough money for the scheme, and three years later demolition proper began. A new voice in the conservation struggle was heard, possibly for the first time in York, when the Society for the Protection of Ancient Buildings met in the city and opposed the loss of the church.

The ruins of St. Michael-without-Walmgate show it to have been quite a substantial church. This drawing, possibly by Francis Place, dates from about 1700, and the remains of the church were presumably cleared away later in the century.

The last medieval church to be demolished in York was St. Mary Bishophill Senior, which came down in 1963. It was a pre-Conquest foundation and had features from most periods, including a brick tower of 1659. Parts of the building were reerected in the newly built Church of the Holy Redeemer on Boroughbridge Road. Canon Bell, writing more than fifty years ago when the church was even then redundant, spoke of its "considerable dignity and beauty", and its removal from this important site within the walls is to be regretted.

The picture reproduced here is the original line and wash drawing by Francis Bedford for 'The Churches of York', which he published with the help of William Monkhouse in early Victorian times.

The view along Petergate used to be rounded off by medieval Christ Church. Even early pictures of the church show that parts of the building had been shaved away for road widenings. The ultimate in road widening came in 1937, when the church was demolished and King's Square took its present shape. The building had been much renewed in the nineteenth century. The tower was a familiar landmark and appeared in many city views.

York is not a city of vistas but more of sudden surprises. Instead of a view across King's Square from The Shambles there was a glimpse of Christ Church instead. The robust Victorian facade and shopfront on the left has been replaced by an unobtrusive neo-Georgian housefront, but the half-timbered building behind remains.

This was the old St Sampson's, showing how little was left of the medieval church before the Victorians rebuilt it. In turn the Victorian church was transformed into an old people's centre in 1974.

A favourite subject for eighteenth and nineteenth century artists was the area of Layerthorpe Postern. Water, a bridge, trees, an old church, half-timbered cottages, and ancient fortifications gave them all they wanted for a picturesque composition. Only the church and part of the wall remain in this now chiefly industrial area where an artist today would probably be choked by petrol fumes before he'd finished his picture.

Adjacent to St. Andrewgate and Goodramgate is Bedern, until 1850 accessible only from the latter. This was the area occupied by the Vicars Choral, whose principal job it was to sing the Minster services. Ridsdale Tate's drawing of 1916 shows the priests' chapel as it was - and as it remained until the 1960s, when its tilt towards the street alarmed the Minster authorities, who turned it into a ruin. Ironically in another twenty years time the medieval hall of the Vicars Choral was rescued from the middle of Victorian factory development, expertly restored, and put to use as a city guildhall. On the facing page, as these early nineteenth century drawings show, Bedern had become one of the quaintest areas of the city - and one of the slummiest. The top drawing, by George Nicholson, is of the South side of the street, and the properties shown could well have incorporated some of the medieval houses of the Vicars Choral. The lower drawing, by Henry Cave, is a continuation of this side of the street towards Goodramgate with the priests' chapel on the right. All the houses on both sides of the street have long since gone.

Pritchett's very handsome Salem Chapel was a fitting end to Georgian St. Saviourgate, now blocked off by an office development that ruins the vista down the street and dwarfs the houses. Acoustically the chapel was said to be excellent, and there were hopes it might become a much needed city centre concert hall.

Almost all the inner city non-conformist chapels have disappeared. The austere Friends Meeting House, still with the furniture originally designed for it, was pulled down in 1981 after a life of 164 years. The atmosphere of prayer and worship was felt strongly in this simple room, now replaced.

Left

Many old York pubs have disappeared this century, though ironically their olde-worlde charm is something breweries try to recreate in hygenic new materials. Most of what mattered in Skeldergate was pulled down after the war. This spacious early nineteenth century house, with Victorian ground floor windows, looks as though it's beginning to lose its balance. As The Elephant and Castle it was finally cleared away in the 1960s.

Facing page

The Plumbers Arms in Skeldergate, which came down in the mid 1960s, was a sad loss. Its unique facade was a favourite with artists and photographers. It is now rebuilt, further back, in Wild West log cabin style and renamed The Cock and Bottle. The elegant facade of the 1816 Albion Chapel can be seen no longer either, as it was removed in 1979, in spite of sensible schemes for alternative use. The chimney on the extreme left was on the house John Carr built for himself. This, too, came down after the war.

GRAND BAZAAR
HOLIDAYS
ESQUIMAUX
FAMILY

Left

Looking as if it has outgrown the house, this monumental classical doorway was in The Queen's Head, Fossgate. This pleasant jettied pub came down in 1964 and was replaced by a flat wall with windows.

Facing page

The Black Bull was another familiar part of York's streetscape. It was pulled down in 1949 and replaced by an inoffensive brick building which does nothing to invite you round the corner as The Black Bull did.

BLACK
BULL
HOTEL
BLACK BULL
ROOM

The White House in Bedern, a stylish late seventeenth century building, was one of those to go when the area was redeveloped in Victorian times. By the time this picture was painted it looks as though the house was divided into tenements and struggling to maintain its respectable air. H. Waterworth, a prolific recorder of local views, was the artist.

One of the most colourful and exuberant buildings in York was the old George Hotel in Coney Street. An inn which bore the sign of the Bull had stood on this site, but in 1614 the landlord, Thomas Kaye, had bought the property and both rebuilt and renamed it. Many famous people have lodged there. Henry Cave drew this view of the inn's oldest part which would have been one of the city's best loved treasures had it survived. In 1868 Leak and Thorpe bought most of the property, pulled it down, and established their store on the site. The gateway and one of the corner pillars which led to the inn yard still remain.

One survival of the George Hotel, nothing short of miraculous, is the main doorway. This probably was the entrance to the Bull Inn which stood on the site in the Middle Ages. It was then reused in the 1614 rebuilding, and when this property was demolished the door was carted away to do much humbler service as a summerhouse behind Holgate Lodge. It finally found a resting place in the Yorkshire Museum, where it is kept in store.

An 1855 ground floor plan of the George Hotel in Coney Street reveals the scale of loss. What all the rooms looked like, and what sort of atmosphere there was, we are never going to know.

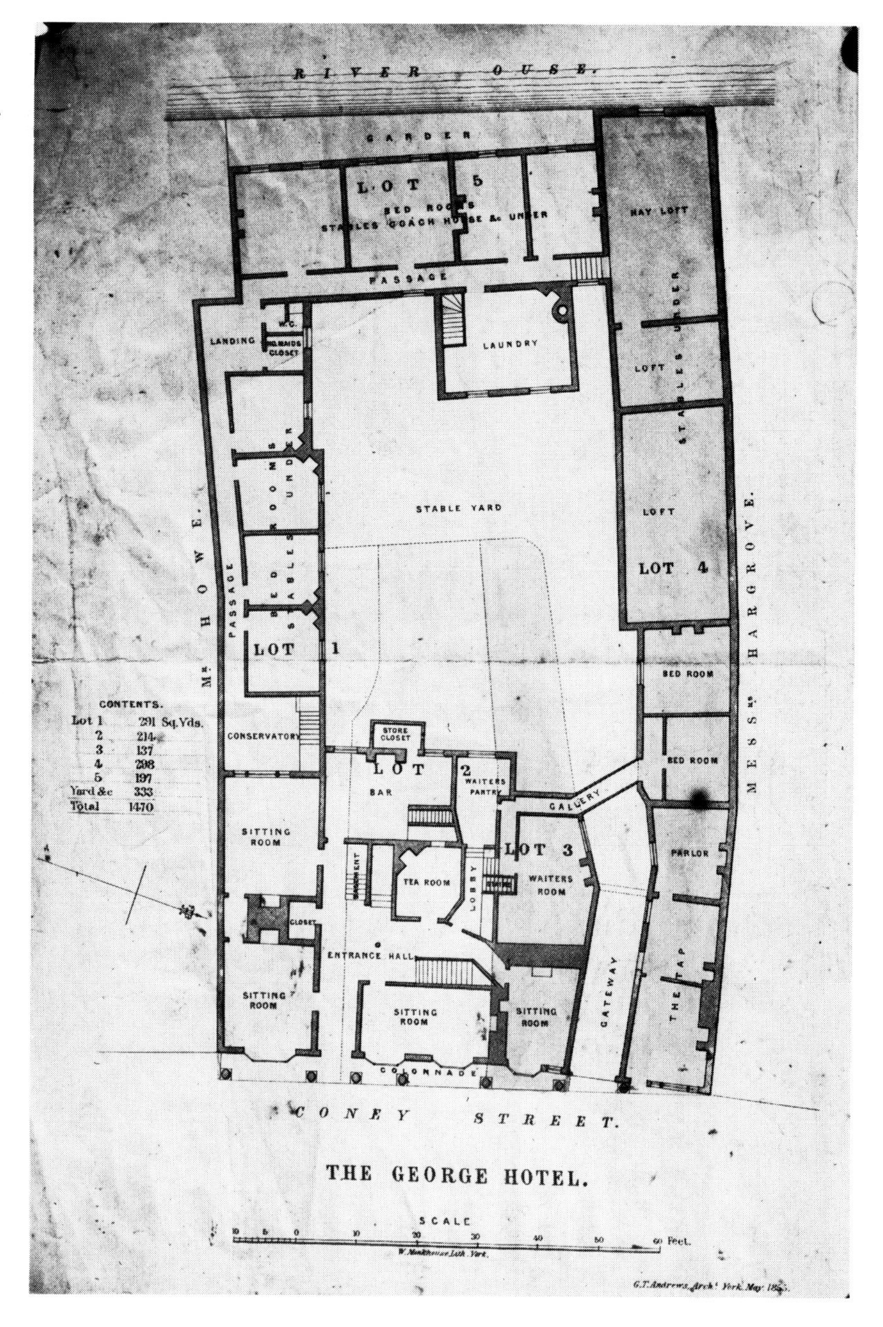

A photograph which records one of York's most handsome hotels, and another showing shops to the side of it. Harker's was a fitting neighbour for the Mansion House, and whereas St. Helen's Square might well be regarded as a planning gain, the loss of a Georgian building of this quality can only be regretted. The hotel interiors were as fine as the facade suggests they would be. All came down in 1929.

'From a Parlour of the York Tavern York. April 6th 1827'.

The York Tavern became Harker's Hotel, and later still removed ground completely to become the Chase Hotel on Tadcaster Road. For the same viewpoint today you'd have to cling to the top of the civic Christmas tree in St. Helen's Square. Even then you'd get a very different picture. The splendid half-timbered house on the left has gone, as have all the fine Georgian shopfronts. The two properties at the end of Stonegate (now Banks Music Shop) have been remodelled, the gable of the one built up at this side to join its larger neighbour, and the building facing them has lost a storey.

Between 1859 and 1864 the approach to the West front of the Minster was transformed. Henry Cave's drawing shows it as it was. Lop Lane, the narrow road leading to the gateway into the Close, was considered "mean" and at a time when vistas and opening up views were all the rage nearly all the properties in this view were enthusiastically condemned. In what was a sort of forerunner to compulsory purchase, Dean Duncombe started a public subscription to purchase properties so they could be demolished. That was the end of another York street. Duncombe Place was created, and it made the next move possible, pushing Deangate through from here to Goodramgate, now so much regretted. It was the end, too, of properties in the foreground. Of all the houses shown only the Red House, on the left, remains, but without its railings or garden. On the right the famous coaching inn Bluitt's, or Etridge's, was pulled down in 1859 and offices created on the site.

Once York Minster had a Close, entered by four gates. Peter Gate was one, stretching across the narrow road from the corner of High Petergate to what is now Duncombe Place, where it joined a row of cottages that attached themselves to St. Michael le Belfrey. (It can be made out in the picture on the preceding page). Seen through the larger arch is Peter Prison, which dealt with offenders in the Liberty of Minster Yard, and had its own officers for doing so. The main room was the Court, called Hall of Pleas, entered by the flight of stone steps seen in the picture. Jonathan Martin, the Minster incendiary, was one of the last people to be held here. The gateway came down in 1827, the prison some years later. This drawing was made in 1895 by G. H. Fowler Jones, presumably based on some earlier picture.

A fine watercolour by H. B. Carter shows the new road through to College Street after the removal of Peter Gate. A pretty cottage still gets itself in the picture, obscuring the full view of St. Michael le Belfrey. This one, and the more elaborate half-timbered example on the right of the painting, presumably went at the time Little Blake Street was wiped off the map.

The entry to St. Helen's Square from Lendal was once narrower because of these old houses, which were done away with in 1883. In fact no building in this view remains. The Post Office was established on this site in the reign of Queen Anne. The 1840s' building shown here was replaced by the present Post Office in 1884, a year after Tom Dudley painted this view.

The Queen's Hotel in Micklegate contained the richest early Georgian interiors in York, hiding them in a typically English way behind a plain exterior. Its disappearance was claimed to be the city's biggest architectural loss since the war. For a long time planners, conservationists, and the firm who'd bought the property argued over whether it could be saved or not. Practically a whole generation has grown up knowing this just as an empty site. The savable parts of the interiors were removed, and if they haven't deteriorated in store, it is said they are to be reinstated whenever the site is developed.

The gateway and Lodge to the Museum Gardens used to be of the Doric order like the museum itself, (and one suspects better proportioned than this wood engraving shows). Built about 1830, when the museum was opened, the entrance formed a more appropriate approach to what is York's most splendid Grecian building, the Yorkshire Museum. The architect was William Wilkins, who deliberately eschewed the Gothic style, noting that, 'You have such Gothic at York that any design in the same style must appear trifling.' Whether he also produced the design for the Gateway and Lodge is not known. His judgement seems right when we consider the present inoffensive little Gothic Lodge and gates, which are no substitute for the earlier grand and prominent classical design they replaced about fifty years later.

Like a view of Toy Town, this 1805 print shows a quaint setting for Bootham Bar. Now all the houses in the picture have gone, and the Bar itself is the poorer for the loss of its splendidly rugged barbican.

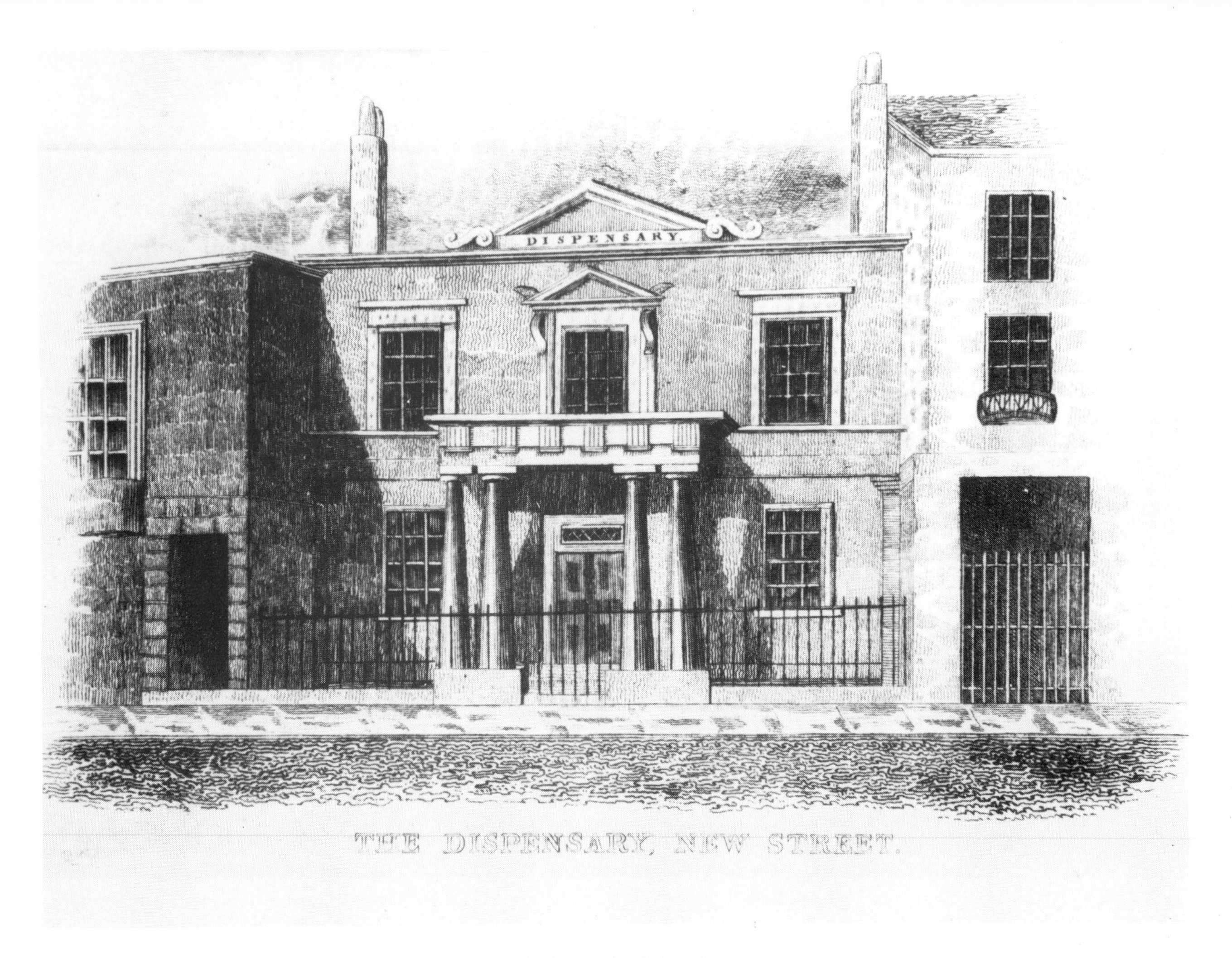

In 1788 The York Dispensary was founded to minister to the needs of the sick poor of the city. It was started first in a hired room in the Merchant Adventurers' Hall, then moved to St. Andrewgate, and in 1828 to these handsome purpose-built premises in New Street, now no more. In the summer of 1832 the doctors here were at their busiest administering twelve hours a day to victims of the cholera epidemic. Subsequently the Dispensary was moved yet again, this time to the bright red brick buildings in Duncombe Place still bearing the name.

The York County Hospital.

The bold design of the County Hospital on Monkgate, founded in 1740 after the city had gone without a hospital for two hundred years. The large Victorian building which replaced it (now converted to offices) was erected further back from the road in 1851, and then work on taking down the old hospital began. During archaeological excavations in 1982 the foundations of this early building were uncovered.

a

b

c

d

When a building vanishes from the street scene most of us miss the familiar facade, but with that also go the many minor pleasures of the interior, staicases, doors, and panelling. Some are saved to be reused, but most are carted away as scrap. Here are pictures of some of those features many will never have seen.

a. A simple Georgian staircase at 24 Monkgate, the handrail sweeping down and round with graceful assurance.

b. A Chinese staircase at the top of 19 Pavement. The house this came from is shown on page 76.

c. A pencil drawing of a very fine Jacobean staircase at Barclays Lodgings in York. What happened to it is unknown.

d. A closeup of the early eighteenth century staircase at 4 Micklegate, lost when the Co-op extended their premises in blockbuster style in the 1960s.

At the top, the quaint Jacobean ceiling at 18 Micklegate, another property swallowed up by the Co-op development. The house formed part of one of the largest timber-framed buildings in York, and might have been built about 1590 as a major inn. Below, the painted room at 17 Micklegate, photographed shortly before its demolition, was a demonstration of the skill of the Victorian painters and decorators who operated from here. The room was at the back of the property and remained unknown to most. The house itself was basically fifteenth century, with many later alterations.

Above

Joshua Cowling painted this view of York's first Gas Works, between Monkgate and the Foss. The company was formed in 1823, though the price of gas remained so high that many people continued to use oil to light their houses. The pretty brick entrance buildings, looking like the lodge gates of some rural estate, survived until the 1980s.

Facing page

a. The quality of Georgian craftsmanship displayed here in a mid-eighteenth century overmantel from 27 Trinity Lane, photographed during demolition in the 1960s.

b. The original Georgian glasses cupboard from the Board Inn, Fossgate.

c. Union Terrace, bulldozed out of existence about 1972, had many pleasant minor features, like this cast iron gate, almost certainly produced at the Walker Foundry in York. (John Walker was appointed Ironfounder to Queen Victoria, and though his grandest commissions were in London, much of his excellent work remains in York). An area of attractive small nineteenth century houses, Union Terrace and Clarence Street have become a coach and car park.

d. A Carron grate from Spurriergate, one of hundreds of examples to disappear.

a

b

c

d

Corners are especially vulnerable. Here is Gillygate, seen through Queen Margaret's arch in a cracked early slide. The building on the right, with its elegant first floor window and canted doorway, shows how corners should be turned. Now there is only tarmac where once it stood and traffic and pedestrians battle for the increased roadspace. The unusual windows in the house on the left have now gone too, though the building was recently saved from near dereliction and sympathetically restored. In Georgian times this was the home of Thomas Wolstenholme, carver and maker of composition ornament, which was exported as far as America. Sadly all the fine interiors, a showcase of his craftsmanship, have disappeared.

Another corner to vanish was at the junction of Blossom Street with Queen Street, where stood this handsome late Georgian house. An attempt at renaming, which briefly gave York two King Streets, was not successful, though the stone sign can be seen directly below the Blossom Street one.

DOGS NOT
ADMITTED.

Facing page

York's old Guildhall was bombed in 1941 and the replacement building keeps but little more than part of the outer shell. This photograph, taken shortly before the building burned out, shows the main doorway with stained glass window above. None of the stained glass was saved. Most of the windows illustrated scenes from York's past, so that to be inside was like having a colourful History lesson.

Above

The hall of the Merchant Taylors was once approached through this Victorian archway, with earlier adjacent properties. These, and the short Victorian terrace of houses, have been cleared away since the war.

MIDLAND BANK LIMITED
CITY sales

Arguably the finest facade in Parliament Street, this building with its noble banking hall was designed by P. F. Robinson and G. T. Andrews in 1836. The Midland Bank replaced it in 1971 with an ultra-modern structure.

ISAAC POAD & SONS
BRAIME'S
TADCASTER BREWERIES, LTD
CORN
&
POTATO MERCHANTS.
CROMBIE
&
SONS
BILL
POSTING
OFFICE
YORKS
HAMS
&
BACON
CLOVER SEEDS
TURNIP &
MANGOLD SEEDS
HEAD OFFICES & WAREHOUSES 84 & 86. WALMGATE
FLOUR
BRAN
SHARPS
&c.

Facing page

This quaint row of jettied houses in Pavement enclosed Parliament Street and gave it the feel of a market place. Only tarmac marks the spot where they once stood, and Parliament Street now opens into the bleakness of Piccadilly. On the far left house can be seen the battered survival of a canopied and richly decorated doorway, and the closeup shows a detail of the doorway of the neighbouring house. At one time such doorways were a feature of the city's streets. Now only one remains, much restored, and removed to Jacob's Well in Trinity Lane.

Right

York still continues to lose fine buildings - even if it's nobody's fault, as would appear to be the case when this early seventeenth century house in Coney Street was pulled down in 1981. Its treasures and its date were only revealed when demolition was imminent. The fireplace had been covered up for so long that it was free from generations of paint and knocks. The house seemed to be plain nineteenth century work with a later shop front, but behind modern accretions lay the fireplace, decorated beams, and contemporary panelling.

Most of the properties in this wartime picture of Goodramgate have gone, and a huge concrete arcade of shops lumbers round the curve in the road.

This assortment of houses in Trinity Lane is no more, most of the properties being demolished this century so that now the little street is one of the bleakest in York.

J.RYMER
Joiner and
Undertaker

All these houses in St. Andrewgate have gone, disappearing piecemeal until the last remnant of the Georgian terrace, seen in both photographs, could be mopped up. So another York street quietly disappeared since the war, and St. Andrewgate began to look little more than a servicing and car parking area for the stores along Goodramgate. Finally, in 1979 when a group of late seventeenth and eighteenth century houses were pulled down very quickly, work started on developing the whole area - for housing!

Left

A craftsman in architectural ornament, who lived at this house in St. Andrewgate, used its narrow facade to display his skills. Its pretty draped window went the way of most of St. Andrewgate - into demolition trucks.

Facing page

King's Square lost this dignified Georgian house of 1775 and adjacent properties in the 1950s when this side of the square was redeveloped with shops.

KINGS COURT
SHAMBLES

In spite of one's dilapidation, these early eighteenth century houses provided a better entry to Shambles than the Marks and Spencer's loading bays that give a taste of Brobdingnag before Lilliput.

The old Marks and Spencers and the old British Home Stores, both fitting more politely into the streetscape than do their successors.

Coney Street, full of Georgian chic. The elegant ground floor windows have all gone. The central doorway, and the Black Swan above it, were offered sanctuary in the Castle Museum when this famous coaching inn was demolished.

Details of doorways that once enlivened the city's streets some with fantastic carvings and practical hoods.

One of the greatest medieval mansions in York was Davy Hall, or Lardiner Hall, named after the powerful Le Lardiner family. Most of the property was pulled down in 1745, when New Street was created and part of the site given in exchange for St. Helen's churchyard, now the square. Bits presumably still survived into this century, as Ridsdale Tate's sketch shows, though now modern development covers the site. A fragment of the churchyard remains, incongruously sandwiched between shops.

The familiar tower of All Saints Pavement in the background, and in the foreground a ramshackle precursor of The White Swan.

Facing page

Providing emphasis at the corner of Micklegate and St. Martin's Lane, this gingerbread house gave way in the 1860s to a ponderous Italianate building in white brick. Of the earlier property Davies, in his 'Antiquarian Walks Through York', notices: 'On the front of this house, towards Micklegate, we may still discern heraldic devices executed in the plaster, the most conspicuous of which is an achievement, nearly effaced, probably representing the armorial bearings of Queen Elizabeth. The others are the Tudor Rose, and the Bear and Ragged Staff - the well-known badge of the Dudleys. It can scarcely be doubted that this was the residence of some person connected with the Earl of Huntingdon, who was Lord President of the Council of the North during the latter part of Queen Elizabeth's reign, and whose Countess was the sister of the celebrated Robert Dudley, Earl of Leicester.'

Above

Browns Department Store replaced this modest half-timbered house on the corner of St. Sampson's Square and Davygate. The gabled building in the background has gone too.

Both these drawings come from one of George Nicholson's useful sketchbooks, where views often have the immediacy of a snapshot. At the top is another glimpse of a vanished corner of York. The cosy gables of Thursday Market have all gone, replaced by roadway and Victorian brick, and even the tower of St. Sampson's in the background has been substantially rebuilt.

The lower drawing is one of York's vanished guildhalls, Haberdashers Hall, which stood in Walmgate. Though not as grand as remaining guildhalls it was nevertheless an interesting building and its loss is to be regretted.

At the top, this distinctive seventeenth century warehouse in Skeldergate was repaired by the Council as late as the 1960s, and then pulled down. An ideal size for housing or hotels, Benson's Warehouse with its Dutch gables would have cheered up this key site by the river. Nearly facing it, on the other bank of the Ouse, these houses once stood on King's Staith. The little drawing is sketched on a small envelope. Did its artist wish to have a record of the properties before the huge clearance that transformed several acres of the inner city in the 1880s? The little house with the Dutch gable on the right of the picture was the first to go, along with several others on that side of Friargate.

A street that would have completely outshone the Shambles as a tourist attraction was First Water Lane. It had everything – gradient, length, narrowness, plenty of quaint medieval houses, and the river at the bottom. It also had the highest crime rate in the city, and thus in a big Victorian clean-up, with adjacent streets going later, it was removed in its entirety. Artists loved it, and this viewpoint chosen by W. Collingwood, once Ruskin's secretary, was a popular one.

Two Victorian drawings of this eye-catching medieval house in Water Lane. There are vestiges of an elaborate wooden Gothic window and the remains of spandrels forming a handsome porch. In the photograph these had shrunk even further to just stone corbels on either side of the door. Nothing of the house remained above, and now even the stonework has vanished.

Not an ivy-clad cottage from the heart of the country but 159 and 161 Holgate Road before they were replaced by public conveniences.

Ironically the site next to the tallest office block in York was once occupied by the lowest range of almshouses, Dr Colton's. The North Eastern Railway Headquarters loom over them in this photograph of about 1909, the year they were demolished.

Cottages about to disappear for road widening. The top picture shows the patchy row that faced the city walls in Queen Street – to be replaced by an equally patchy wall set further back. The lower picture shows earlier cottages being removed in 1912 from near St. Cuthbert's Church where they helped to give some feeling of place to a now bleak part of the city.

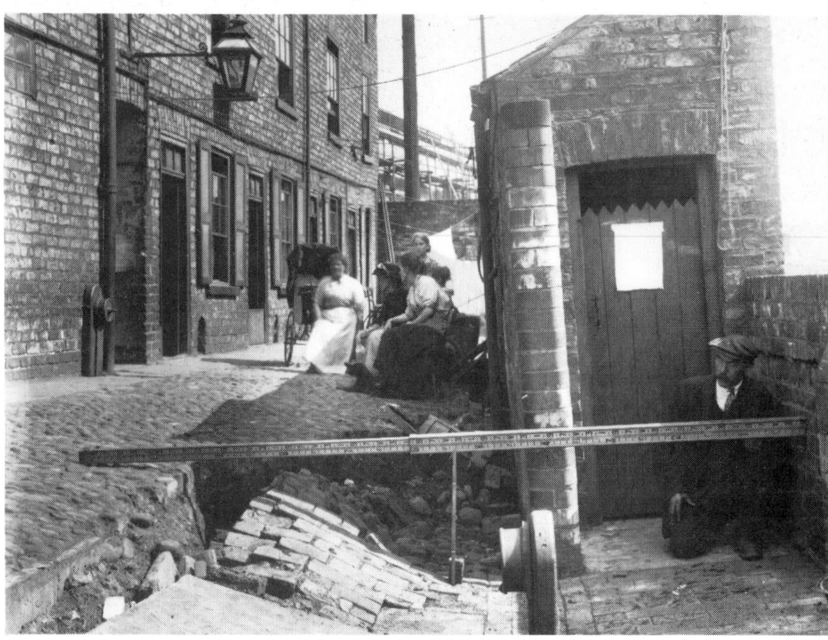

Not all York's vanished buildings are to be mourned. No one will regret the passing of slums like these. The top picture, dated 1912, shows St. Dennis Street with the Cocoa Works on the left. The lower picture, dated 1922, is of a view not yet identified. These photographs, and those on the facing page, come from the city engineer's collection, now housed in the York Archives Office.

Two sides of Waterloo Place, a 'picturesque' slum off Coney Street which must have had one of the craziest rooflines ever seen in York. The buildings look sadly neglected, but how today we would admire the traditional materials used, stock brick, pantiles, cast iron railings, and stone paving.

John Carr's grandstand on Knavesmire, looking like Assembly Rooms that have strayed into the country, provided the elegant focal building for eighteenth century race-goers. In this 1762 print the course seems to be used as a parade ground for fashionable society, rather like the riverside New Walk. Parts of the building remain, swallowed up by ungainly successors on the site.

Few buildings in the city can have had such a brief life as this one, erected in Swiss-chalet style for the Yorkshire Fine Art and Industrial Exhibition in 1866. It covered one and a half acres and was placed in the grounds of Bootham Park Hospital, where it was visited by the Prince and Princess of Wales. Such was the financial success of the venture that enough money was raised to start a fund for a permanent exhibition hall – the present Art Gallery in the appropriately named Exhibition Square. Thus the first building effectively gave life to another.

Facing page

This handsome Georgian building of 1790 was the officers mess in the Cavalry Barracks on Fulford Road. The army redeveloped the site in the 1970s, saving just the Coade stone royal coat of arms from the pediment. The date and name can be seen in the bottom right hand corner.

Right

Two views of the lodge to Nunthorpe Hall or Court which graphically illustrate how buildings are at risk as the city grows. The top photograph shows the lodge keeper and his family in the estate's Victorian heyday, when it still must have looked like a property in the country. By 1925 when the lower picture was taken the building was in a dilapidated condition after part of the estate had been sold off for housing. Bishopthorpe Road with its tramlines is in the foreground. A street sign (South Bank Avenue) has been fixed to the lodge's pediment, part of the property has been lopped off, it has lost a pillar, and has been converted into a shop. It looks thoroughly run down and out of place. Now it has disappeared altogther.

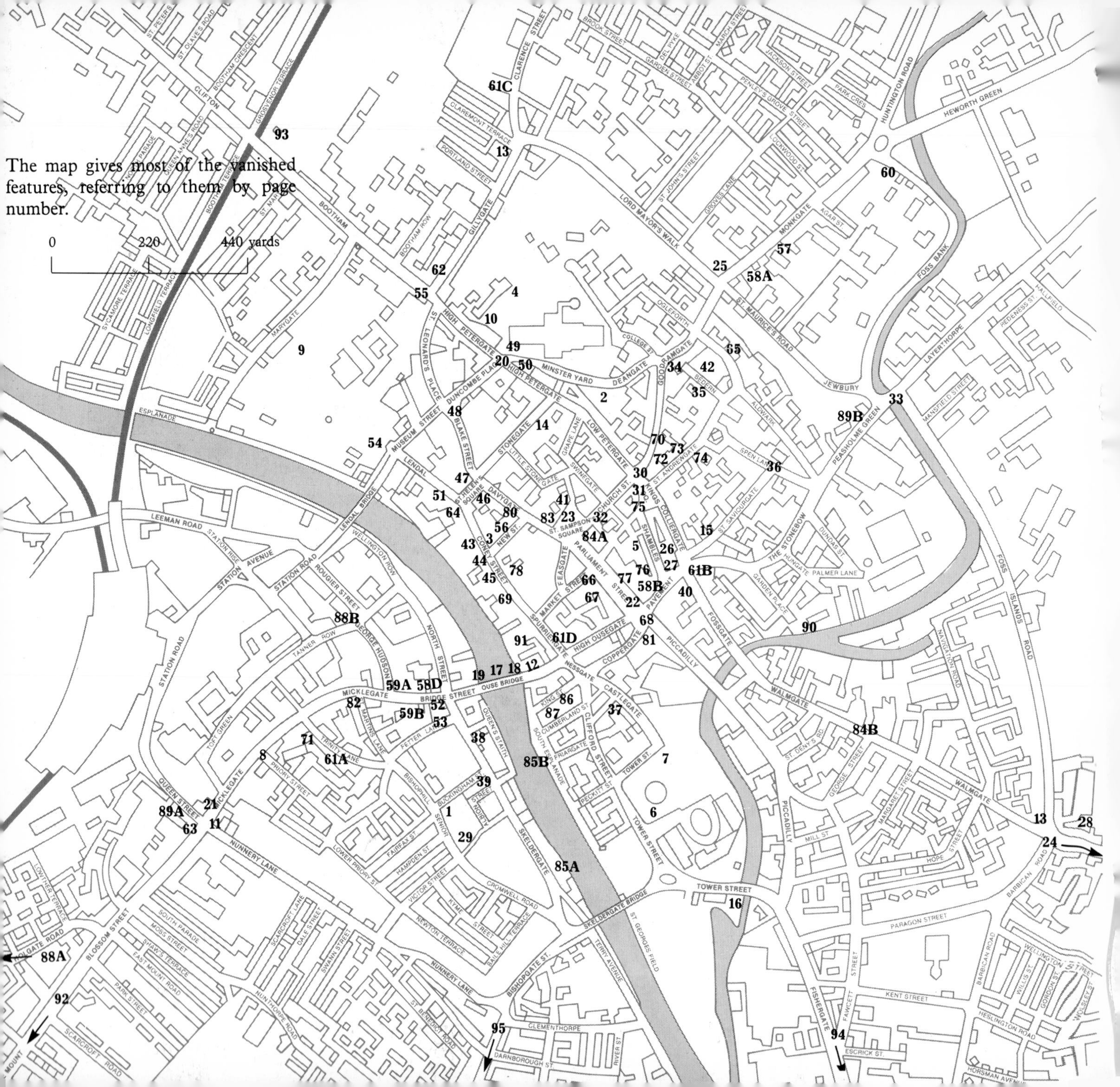

The map gives most of the vanished features, referring to them by page number.